Main

INTO THE WOODS

Anna Robinson

INTO THE WOODS

ENITHARMON PRESS

First published in 2014
by Enitharmon Press
10 Bury Place
London WC1A 2JL

www.enitharmon.co.uk

Distributed in the UK by
Central Books
99 Wallis Road
London E9 5LN

Distributed in the USA and Canada
by Dufour Editions Inc.
PO Box 7, Chester Springs
PA 19425, USA

ISBN: 978-1-907587-56-6

Enitharmon Press gratefully acknowledges the financial support of
Arts Council England, through Grants for the Arts.

British Library Cataloguing-in-Publication Data.
A catalogue record for this book is available
from the British Library.

Designed in Albertina by Libanus Press
and printed in England by
SRP

ACKNOWLEDGEMENTS

This book began life thanks to a Hawthornden Fellowship. There are a few lines in the poems that were 'borrowed' from Edna O'Brien's novel *In the Forest* (Phoenix). The shape of the book comes from Christopher Vogler's book *The Writer's Journey* (Pan). In addition there are references from Sara Maitland's *Gossip from the Forest* (Granta) and John Coulter's *Norwood Past* (Historical Publications). I am grateful for the help of the staff of Lambeth Archives and Chester Archives and Local Studies Office.

I am also grateful to Martyn Crucefix, Jacqueline Gabbitas and Mimi Khalvati and her workshop group for feedback and encouragement. Similarly, to artist Lesley Logue, with whom I collaborated on two related projects – Book Works at the University of East London and The Written Image at Edinburgh Printmakers and the Scottish Poetry Library.

To Kate, Elsie and Grace – the grandmothers in the woods

CONTENTS

I

The Ordinary World

CITY SNOWSCAPE

As the city was about to fall
under the weight of snow
I would sit and sing
about myself and my shadow self.
But here it doesn't seem
so much a song, more
orchestrated shouting
and my shadow is harsh
and looms over the slush
blocking out the sun
from the underworld,
it fools insects into thinking
they are dead and gone.

FROM THE CHAIR

In my book it says the wild wood is myth.
It was never there; there were no branches
curling out to touch the wild girl as she passed.

There may well have been this girl – there were
girls and women; some were fierce, some fortune
tellers with coined scarves and cunning ways.

There were four widows, called Mary, who bought
plots when it was sold. When the Archbishop
himself decreed the woodlands dead and gone.

But even if the girl was wild, her hands
were not the shape of oak leaves and her smell
was more cold tea than earth. I read all this

in the corner, in the brown chair, head turned
so when I lift my eyes, they alight on the wall
and I see the cobwebs the duster missed.

ON THE MARSH

There's a chestnut stall on the corner,
always in the shadow of the rank sky –
varnish works, soap, candle, vinegar
works, shot tower – there's a man
saying *they'd search you every day,*
but they never found what I had
and another man saying *'course*
it was rough, but they wasn't wicked.

He knows about wood and in his shed
keeps a range of tools: claw hammers,
for floorboards, pins for tintacs, a lump
for whatever needs bashing, all made
of wood by him when he was young
and they never found what he had either.

He shines his wood with a polish;
beeswax with shellac. It smells of trees.
He does not do this to be cruel,
he's not wicked, nor all that rough.
A quiet man – bar the cough.

His son doesn't touch the hammers,
just stands on the doorstep smoking
then walks down the Marsh to the end.
There's a man on the corner saying
"I'll tell you the names on this street".

PLAYGROUND

The ground, once black pitch,
is covered in brick dust and little clumps of weeds;
mostly grasses and small round leaved things

that creep as far as they can.
In one corner, yellow stars stand tall in a mass
of flowering grasses, forming a little garland.

In the wall, an unused
arrow slit makes a portal for black birds.
A cast iron joist supports a jutting thing.

There's something, in the red
stone, the colour of old snow, and odd spots of lichen.
Here – the weeds do hesitate –

there's nowhere the wind won't go
and all their heat goes into making that long crawl
to bunch in the sheltered spot.

II

The Call To Adventure

SORE EYES

There's a rowan tree outside the park.
The lady of the mountains, when
she arrived in the city, would burn it
in the spring time in her fireplace.

After she'd breathed in the fire smoke
she'd charge out of her flats and dance
like a nutter round the stones in the fountain.

She'd gargle it after singing in the pub made
her voice coarse and vulgar. Her berries
are bitter, bitter as ink, her tongue reborn,
and her bark, no worse than her bite!

FROM THE CHAIR II

I read my book all day and all night.
In my book it says *my heart yearns*
and as it says – so it is –
        a slow hurt spreads.

It says *we smiled at the thought,*
my mouth-sides lift. The chair
I sit in is brown and old;
        once it lived at home.

I would sit there with our dog,
my Mum would sit there, my sister
would hang upside down there because
        she was that kind of child.

In this book there's a wood and a child.
She likes running through the bracken.
It whips her round the legs. She likes
        the bright red weals.

A HAUNTING

In the station there's a train not for riding,
it's carved out of wood; has an engine,
two carriages, details of wheels, windows,
signage – all chiselled with a steady hand.

It's on a wooden rail, going nowhere.
The train is full of mud, right to the top, planted
with petunias, all climbing like they can't wait
to get out, back to the fields, to the onion patch.

The town is dark and dormant. Night has fallen
on the wooden toy train, bars and shops
all dark and shut; the room where I sleep – dark.

Out there John's grave stone, hand carved by him,
the family names, his name the only one
not chiselled, not by his hand, nor anyone else's.
His own son preferring the fields to the craft.

LILY IN SNOW

It was the snow that made her white and made
the world white and she and the world were lost
on the horizon. Outside the first mist
gathers as vapour over the city. She leaves
no tracks as she comes and goes; breathing her thin
brittle breath. Somewhere there's a smear
of dark above the rooftops. Somewhere above
the snow that quiets the city, the darkness spreads.

INTO THE WOODS

In my sleep the woods are calling
so I dress and go, stand awhile
between the trees; a mass of people
appear around me as if out of a fog

dressed in rags, their arms piled high
with kindling. I ask them what they want
of me, *Nothing* they say, I ask
Who are you? *Just ourselves, nothing more,*

your bones, nothing to see or understand.
Are you here for me? I ask and *No,*
they say, *We're just here.* And then – *We'll leave*
a trail for you to follow, if you must.

III

Refusing The Call

ROWAN

There's a stone seat up here
on the precipice. If you sit
still, dangle your feet, you're queen
of the woods, lady of the mountains,
you could cure sores, bad throats
know all about what's sacred
and what's not, but if you slip
it's a long fall to a cold wet grave.

LYING IN

I'm lying in the gutter on the Marsh,
beneath me runs a rivulet of coffee
coloured water that stinks so rank I know
I may never get up again. I'm not
cold. I can see myself, part of me

has flown, is looking down and sees
I'm covered in a blanket of lined paper.
Scrawled across in a large untidy hand –
last night we had fish fingers for dinner.

NOT FROM THE BROWN CHAIR

Now I will not read and the brown
chair sits alone doused in an old throw.
There are always piles of things on it
so no-one who visits would sit there.

It faces away from the others, away
from the telly towards the unlit hearth;
it has no cushions and even the cat
prefers the ruts of the well worn sofa.

Under the unhoovered carpet – floorboards
spitting nails, and under them, mice
scratching earth, tunnelling down and out
through the dark, towards the living marsh.

THE NUTCRACKER

He didn't want to use a sledgehammer
to crack it or a blow torch to warm it.
The ice was spread thick over
what was once a river, a sand bronze
river running south through a wood.

They fooled it, had it tamed and banked
before covering it over with small
grey streets. His chest is wheezy. The ice
runs under his feet, his house, his stove.

WATCHING

There I am, in that cottage, right beside
the wood, and gazing out at every given
moment, I watch the midpoint, just below
the canopy for signs of birds and now
and again into the thick of it for something
that might stir. While you sleep, or bathe
or cook, I wander out – always intending
to unslip the latch of the garden gate,
rehearsing the movement of my hand each time,
how its metal will resist me, planning
how my hand will move to ease it through.

I will walk your garden path, my eye
adjusting to the horizon, to the sky,
almost not looking at the trees until
I'm there at the gate and then my hand
will fail. I never do enter the woods.
Always refusing and I don't know why.
Did I think you'd wake and find me gone,
believe I'd slipped through some hole in the world,
leaving just my luggage for the landfill.

IV

Meeting With The Mentor

THE BOOK OF MARY

I sit in the chair, reading, feet tucked
beneath me and my book is telling me
about the wild wood. The book is endless
and my breath slows and all seems to stop.

I sit holding it, turning the pages,
read and the voice of the book is my voice
its presence is the weight of it in my hands
the dryness of its paper under my fingers.

Sometimes I think I hear the postman enter;
sometimes the upstairs neighbour's phone,
but mostly nothing intrudes and the path
into the wood opens. A while passes

before I start to hear the slight blurred
shift of a deeper note, a lack of tremor,
a voice with a different grain. And my fingers,
are they holding or being held? And then

she steps out – the storyteller. I look up
from the book, eyesight blurred and she says
I am Mary and once I owned a wood.

MEETING THE WOODSMAN

Yes, well, there's a straggly hedge, yew,
box or something and other things I barely
recognise. There's murmuring somewhere
and tapping yet I can see no-one, bird or animal.
What is so wonderful about being a woodsman?

There's hikers in my wood, with maps, a B&B,
a child and a white dog both knee deep in mud.
To the dog, the mud won't stick, his coat's so coarse
but the child is heavy with it and cannot run.
There's a clearing on higher ground, called
the Donkey Green, with a coffee stall and once,
a tombola. There are clouds above. Down below –
after the yew trees, a row of shiny black
motorbikes, each more loved than the last.

THE GIRL GLIMPSED

It was the same child I always
bring to the woods, the one with red
cheeks, who wants to see the deer
and never does 'cause she can't
keep still. She is wearing a red
duffle coat and shrunken ski-pants,
short socks and black plimsolls.
Her calves are red with cold.

She has got herself dressed
and her mother would have a fit
if she saw her, the trousers fished
out of the bin for the fourth time.
The child runs in and out of the bracken
like she's pure air.

CAVE CANEM

Eyes and no eyes; it's like this: you pass
through a low doorway unmarked by shells
or crosses. At the end of the tunnel, a small
round light shines in from the world – it's a porthole
to a gorge. You can look but don't try to jump.

Then, to the right, carved into the limestone
boxes for boxes for the dead. I could label
them: Kate, Grace, Bill and Mum, but don't,
because they're empty. They can't hold the dead,
don't even try. Just stare – like dark eyes

in a dark hollow space. The dog, sleeping
on the end of my bed, dreams something
that makes her tremble so much the whole bed
shakes me awake. She is long gone now,
clean of her bones, beyond a doorway, deep
in the woods, in a shroud of leaves and twigs.

V

Crossing The Threshold

SUMMER FETE – BOX HILL

Blue, yellow, pink; a hundred yards
of bunting on the donkey green,
the tombola, the lady with the knitted
animals, the man selling photos
of clouds, and him, the toddler, naked
but for his nappy, dancing to the band.
The smell of warm Box hangs in the air,
mingles with beer, tea, vanilla and ginger.

And all those motor bikes riding on clouds
of steam on the high road through the woods,
across the Donkey Green, round and back
from the café to the look-out post. See this,
Devil's Dyke – only twenty-six miles.

FIELD WALKING

I was left alone in a big field facing
North. I began to walk through thinking
now I will learn what it feels like
to walk through a field, now
I will remember. As I walked,
the grasses whipped me and I grew wet,
a rising damp that clammed me up. Then
I remembered the Donkey Green and the street
of grey houses, the tower and bracken,
spikier than grass but just as wet.
It is this field, just here, and it borders the wood.

LISTENING TO THE WOODS

If only the birds would stop singing
then I'd know if what I heard
was the true sound of the forest,
of creatures moving through their world,
of wind rushing through yew and box.
On the long path, the yew has bent
over itself and is a temple,
a bower, and on the long path,
the lights shine from the bikers' cafe.

THE PALE

It was then the wood lost its old name,
each letter dropping day by day along
with its leaves and animals. I found one
in my hearth, it had fallen down the chimney,
B for Beith, for babies' cradles, for birch whips
to beat and cleanse. A good letter
to get when you need a fresh start.

VI

Allies And Tests

WALKING THE WOOD

It was like breaching through net,
fine, spider-made, and all day
along the river path I felt
I was breaking through with each step.
The fine strong hairs of their webs
across my cheek, not the heart
of the web, more the long guy ropes
that tether it to the bracken
and I kept chanting – *Oh Heart*
of the Web, Heart of Bracken,
give me the strength to persevere.

THE WOODSMAN'S NEST

He was growing a moustache.
It was fragile at first, patchy,
but is now full, like an old librarian's.
His house is in the centre
of the wood and has cracked windows.
Small birds peck the frames looking
for insects and roost in the ivy.
The pigeons are eating this house,
pecking it down, brick by brick.
One day it will fail to hold.

THE LONELIEST CHILD

Born on a precipice in what was once a forest,
the trees knew her well and she loved to run
through the valley bottom, through bracken,
along the river, listening to the distant sound
of dogs swimming. She didn't know how to
seek out company, not even that of the dogs
and when the woods were chopped down,
she hardened to coal. Since the Clean Air Act
she's lost, doesn't know what to do with herself.
From time to time you'll smell her brackishness
or see one small scaly leaf at the base of a flower.

BACK ON THE MARSH

There's something in the kitchen that's not right.
The doorstep's not washed, the hearth not whitened.
No neat row of crosses and they have definitely
not been rubbed with oak leaf. The door creaks
and I know at least there's food in the pantry.
What will happen if the fog returns
and the brittle ice reaches the city?

There are splinters of glass all over the floor.
I step towards the corner to get the broom,
sweep it away. The bracken is growing under
the tower, even as I sweep, nothing
I can do. The glass in the dust pan
foretells a messy old man who will come when
the tower falls, when all that glistens is gone.

VII

The Approach

FIRST

there was a snow-storm, then trees
and eyes and no eyes and a nest that sat
in my hand. The year spun by with all
its doings. I sat by the whitened
hearth waiting for the face at the window,
staring the other way but knowing
it would come. Someone came and went;
they said the word 'Christmas', I remember.
I lit a candle then and placed it in the window
and the flame glowed, basking in its own reflection

Across the street was a row of shops. Each one
had a low lying window – with a narrow
wooden ledge upon which you could rest
your foot to tie a shoelace. In one window
there were groceries, in another
knitted things, knitted from the softest,
rarest wools. They were not cheap and came
from sheep and goats who roamed the woods
on the foothills. Each was named for the weather
that birthed her, Fog, Evening Mist, Shower,
Drizzle, Spit. Each was fed on meadowsweet
and the down of finest thistles. Each was loved
as was her right. They were only for sale
to those deemed responsible enough. The street
was painted grey, a dusky duck-egg grey.

THISTLES

I'm your sister and nothing can change that.
There we are walking up Box Hill
with Shaun, Christian and Jack, Mum gone on
in a cab, her knees not up to the steep climb
of the short path and Jack, stripped off to his nappy,
hating the mud on his clothes and as Shaun
is carrying the picnic hamper, you and I carry
Jack, in turn; our bobbing faces purple,
our hair wild and straggly, straining under
his weight. On the way back down we're smaller,
Mum is lighting matches to show us the way.

I WAS AWAKE ALL NIGHT WITH THE BELLS RINGING

So, I sat in my nest of leaves under
a tree and read, thinking of the brown
chair at home, its velvet old and dusty.
All night I sat like this, and between
the pages of the book called *In the Forest*:
meringue crumbs, dropped by its last reader.
Was she a good sleeper – that reader? I baked
the child meringues for one birthday, back
home in the city. It was night time and we
were sat in the back yard on a new moon.
I lit candles so the child could see their peaks.

IN THE HAZE OF THE SHELTERING MOUNTAIN

It appears that Mrs Dawson is a woman
of sense. She wears flat shoes with a good grip
and warm clothes of the sort that weather can't
easily penetrate. She's scraped her long hair
into a ponytail, to keep it out of the way.

She carefully steers herself down the steep
slope to the river to see what she can find
in those sandy waters to make art with,
then she sees them; two little girls in short skirts
and slingbacks, quarter of the way up the mountain
all goatlike sure-footedness. She cries.

VIII

The Ordeal

AN ENDLESS TALE

The trees have grown whips, which reach out
slapping my face as I stumble blindly,
not quite falling, clutching, sliding, heels
digging in the mud, cold slime under
my bare feet, best dress torn, legs bleeding,
nettle rash all over my arms. Mouth
full of web, wrapped around my tongue.
Nostrils full of the scent of rotten
wood and mud. Then this ground gives way
and I plunge down the slope to the wild, wild river.

I am stacking shoes in a shoe shop.
It's one I used to work in, in a long grey
street. The shoes must be stacked the way
the manageress wants, it must be done
before tea. Someone comes in looking
for navy sandals, which I must find before
I continue stacking, then the phone rings
it's another branch asking if I can send
them beige slippers and all the time I should
be stacking. I'm falling behind. The manageress
is a cruel woman, young but with a straight
nose and grey eyes. She would never
sack me – enjoys wielding the whip too much.
Her web is taut and her tongue a rope of nettle.

I have banged my head on the rocks. The light
is dazzling – everything around me in sharp
focus, the way it was the day mum died.
Am I dead? Is this the white tunnel you walk
down to the light? Is this Pale Death?

DEAR DAD

When I was a child and had lost all hope
of you returning; I slept and dreamt Andromeda
at the end of a telescope; a dark, dark sky
and dots of light in a dense untranquil sea.

I couldn't make it end, even after waking,
if I closed my eyes she'd be there again, trapped
between her sea and dots of light and I'd cry,
silently, so's not to wake anyone.

And now I've seen her again, this time
for real, in a clearing, the distance seems
wondrous and with refraction she's silver
and you, your voice is fading . . .

MISTLETOE

If he had a woman beside him now
she would bring in a basin of hot water.
She would cradle his sore head and bandage
it with rowan bark, she would bake
with vanilla and ginger, healing all
the hurt in him and his poor broken
house. She'd play mother to the forest
and all the grey would fade like evening time.

LILY DEAD

It's only rain dropping out of a gutter
but it's slow enough to be her heart,
her tiny silent heart – if you could hear it;
and her dead now, not dead and buried
but burnt and scattered, the deed done
far from anywhere she knew and my heart
hanging like a thing caught in a tree.
Oh Flawless Heart of the Wind, bring her home.

HARVESTING

They are here, the wild girls, I can hear them
if I keep still, hold my breath. I can smell
them, all mushroom and salty piss; at last,
now, catch a glimpse of one – maybe two –
leaping between the trees. As I hold still
in my hide, the first emerges into the clearing.

She is collecting fallen things, conkers,
acorns, seeds – stuffing them in a large
ragged bag made of leaves. Her hands
are the colour of unripe acorns, with long filthy
nails. Her hair is autumnal and in her eyes.
She has a small button nose and a mouth
stained with berries. She's creeping towards me,
taut and focussed, like she's hunting me down.

Can she hear my heart beat – or simply smell me?
She stops just before my hide – squats down
and leaves a handful of tiny strawberries. Unsure
I don't move, is she trying to trick me?
Then I remember, this is my story,
I am the hunter – I blink, make my move,
she's gone. The berries are sweet, they're mine.

IX

The Reward

PART OF THE FURNITURE

There was a white linen cloth wound around
each of our hands. Around that was honeysuckle
to bind us to the tree and then she came and built
her nest – it took her eight days, eyes never
seeming to shut as she lined it with grass and moss –
we couldn't move – bound to the spot as we were.

When it was done she laid her eggs, four small
blue eggs, and sat on them for two full weeks.
I was exhausted but if we so much as blinked
she would hiss and peck, so we kept still until
the birds hatched and until, in another two weeks,
                                        they flew.

AUTUMN

As he lies there in his crumbling house
he drifts into a restless gluey sleep,
dreams of wispy clouds and long paths.
On waking, not that refreshed, he feels a hand,
an angel touching him saying, "Get up and eat."
So he strides down, out past the yew trees
and bikes. The bikers in the burger bar
on the edge of the forest make way for him;
as all the lights of the café (the overhead strip
light, the light that kills flies, the neon sign,
the light of the dying sun flooding through
the clean windows) dance their gold refracting
dance in the tea slops on the red formica
table top, he holds his head high, needs no-one.

FALLEN

Watching the fallen tree, thinking myself
round it and round it – I've gone tiny, can weave
my way through its forest of leggy branches.
There is breeze on my light gooseflesh,
now and again a twig swipes. The grass
is patchy and every shade of khaki and reaches
my knee in places. It has a life of its own,
but not so much that it distracts me from
the task. I am here to observe and walk
and in walking, know. I look into
the flaky lizard canopy, down
to the thatch, out to the wider thicket
and see the vague shapes of my story.

OO-ROOOO-COO|OOOO

The smell of grass, pigeons
cooing in a nearby field
their thick necks swelling
for the ritual, and then let
the bowing commence, stretching
higher then low and lower
and the song – oo-roooo-
coo|oooo – sung over and over.
They hold their beaks at right
angles to the ground, and reach
their rainbow. What follows
cannot possibly disappoint.

IN THE HEART OF THE WOOD

Slow as a damp mist I'm aware of a pale white grey,
a brackish smell, that I'm in my body, can move,

open my eyes. I find myself not in the leaves
I'd fallen in but under them and beneath me a hard

grainy surface, not the stuff of the woods. Shifting
myself, I stand and it would seem I'm in the remains

of a broken house. The walls are not quite to my shoulder.
They're covered with white tiles; across most, fine webs

full of grey spiderlings. To one side, a tidy hearth,
marked with neat flowers – not the stuff of the woods.

This house is full of leaves. I follow a wall to a corner
where I find a broom and sweep; see glimpses

of concrete floor, of a black-leaded stove, sticks
of polished wood; hear the whispers of broom on floor,

of leaves against air and what sounds increasingly like
a voice *If seven maids with seven mops swept it*

for half a year… The other side of the wall, the leaves
stir and the face of a dirty child appears. The wild girl.

The hair is brown and life stirs in its knots. For the first
time, I see her eyes, and know that she won't harm me.

Hello, I say, she smiles, says *I know a story,*
tell me a story and I'll tell you yours. I tell her the tale

of an old brown chair that someone once loved for its
stories but as that person's parents grew old and died,

so it lost its charm. Although she dragged it from house
to house, it couldn't regain its place, until one day

a special book arrived that could only be read from that
self-same chair. The person had to work that out

for herself. However, that took time, and, as always
with these kind of things, it was discovered by accident,

when the person, frustrated with the book, flung it
and herself on the chair. The book opened, its light

poured forth. That person, the chair and the book lived
happily ever after. The wild girl laughs and claps

her dirty hands. *I'll tell you a story* – she says. *Cast out
of what remained of their cottage, due to the famine,*

*two children wandered. They knew the layout of the forest –
that knowledge was their birthright. They knew all the tracks,*

*both the old straight ones and the windy ones that led
to the witch's house and although they'd have killed*

*for gingerbread, they didn't go there. Instead they banded
with other children and sought out the sea-lanes, boarding*

*a boat, which took them to a dockyard. From there, they walked
north – following a large star along an icy path.*

One day they came upon a town, where every kitchen
cooked gingerbread and here they settled, and lived

honourable lives with neither fame nor fortune but many
daughters and a few sons to continue their name.

Your go, she says, *My mother, I said, came from the fortress*
in the woods. A good place mostly, with a duck pond,

priest holes, heavy horses, kitchens making treacle.
Outside lurked danger: nuns, cousin Angela and land

that could swallow you whole. Despite this, one day,
she left. Stepping out, she walked across the coastal

plane and went east to the castle. Here she learnt
much, married then travelled south with her husband

to a citadel, whose walls had long been outgrown.
I was born and then, my sister. Our tongues were different

to those of our parents and sometimes this troubled them.
We lived in barns, fields and dockyards; in rooms, flats

and a house. Once we travelled as far as the sea,
and stayed for a year. We grew strong, tall, learnt

to plant a window box. Now, our mother is dead,
our tongues are those of the matriarch, from the fortress

in the woods. But they are flatter, bitten and burnt.
The wild girl claps, laughs as before and dances around

the trees for a bit. *Now I have one for you* – she says –
once upon a time there was a man. He was born

a baby, sound in all, as loud as any baby known.
He was called Bill. Although he was a lovely baby,

his mother was sad. His father had died a month before
and before he could chisel his own name onto

their grave. That was the sad world this Bill was born
into. So, one day he disappeared. No-one

knows where he went, but whilst he was gone he learnt
many things; to read and write, lead a horse to plough,

fight in a war, darn his own socks and sing. One
of his favourite songs was about someone who had

disappeared and who may at any time return.
If he returned in Summer or Winter – it would

be lovely, and the singer would be waiting for him
in a field. But, if he returned in Autumn, it would be

too late. One day, that someone came and found Bill's grave
but as there was no marker, they weren't sure,

The sun is high now, dapples our green clad hides,
comfy in our leaf piles we tell and tell – she tells

me of a library high in the hills, beyond the North wind
where men who mould lead sit and read on brown chairs.

I tell of a girl who finds she's been kidnapped by servants
and raised as one of their own. She tells of a shoemaker descended

from a friend of the King of Scotland. I tell of a woman
who scrubs floors with cold tea and cinders. There is no prince.

The day dims, the shadows sharpen, suddenly she's watchful.
They're coming soon, your people. I'll go now.

She fades down into the leaves on the other side
of the wall. Out of the trees come the brown clad folk,

with their bundles of kindling. They don't seem to see me,
are looking out somewhere beyond. *Hello,* I say,

are you here for me? No, they say, *we are just here.*
This is where we are. Once we lived and now

we're dead, and one day, you'll join us. But, not yet –
take what you need but walk on – out of the forest.

You are not the stuff of the woods. Return to the world.
You need to breathe as they do in the cities. In and out.

We are the out breath. Along with these trees, we make your air.
As long as you breathe we sustain you, when that ceases – we'll come.

At my feet, a pile of kindling, a small brown dog, who licks
my cheek and fades. I stand, take my bundle, walk on.

X

The Road Back

SAME WOODS

that filtered green, the constant leafy murmur,
the crushing hugeness of it, worlds within worlds,
earth and earth and dust. The oak trees beside
the old straight track, the rowan on the mountains,
the yew on the long path, box on the hill,
boxes in the caves, bracken by the river,
under the tower now, Oh Flawless Heart
of the North Wind, breathe for us.

REMEMBERING THE WINDS HE WALKED IN

all of them together, as one massive
shoulder of force, he is propelled
skyward. He thinks this is how
a bird would feel – but he'd be wrong.

SONG OF THE OLD LADY

When I was old and my body almost given up
I lay in my nest in the woods with my head tilted back,
mouth drooped open. My breath was slow, bones
also and somewhere, someone called me Mary.

Mary! he shouted, *get up, shed your leaves –*
shake yourself! but my name is not Mary,
so I ignored him and slept on
and dreamt a city where I would live

could go about my business without the hurt
in me so constant. I'd have a warm bed, high off
the floor, far from the vermin, with soft covers.
A tower perhaps, or a street of grey houses.

GOODBYE WOODSMAN!

What do I do with all my feelings?
They are rising like the moon and sun,
contradict each other, the pain in my back,
the tingle in the ball of my foot, hunger,
my urge to touch animals, to smell
the dank river on drift wood. I'm glad
to be leaving you, Woodsman,
glad to be returning to the city.

THE ROAD BACK

Dust spattering up, the fleeing countryside
runs under the axe of the suburbs, this small
grey street of houses and the toy shops
that sell the stuff of evening. Under the street
the river runs, still sandy beige, fast
across its bed of clay. It dreams of its freedom,
its life and livelihood, carrying the boats
full of oak leaf across to the cold harbour.

XI

The Resurrection

LITTLE BOX

She was in a little box
but I never saw it.
It was never in my hands.
I never smelt or tasted it.
I drank the brackish water
let it run over my face.
I felt for the scaly leaf
at the base of the flower
picked at it, like I pick
at that pox scar on my leg.
She was in that little box
but I never saw the thing.
It was never in my hands

and though she knew it was rash, began
to leap, making her way upstream.
The river was dark but she was brave
and took what help she could, like the lift
she hitched on the rope-cutter's barge.
He took her to where the bridges finish
and on she went, west. But, I know
nothing of the west, so whether
she got there or what she did, I can't say.

FROM THE WINDOW AT DUSK

Clouds – that have been there all day – grey –
from pale concrete to white and a breeze
blowing the seed heads of a dormant geranium
across a window that could do with a clean.

The line that holds the clothes pegs is fading.
I know it's there by the lone peg in the middle
and a sense of something linear stretching hazily
on to the next block. The yellow London brick,

washed clean a decade back, is browning with dusk
and the wind's picking up – banging the seed head –
the clouds are evening out – the block lights just
come on and I start to fill the window – swept

hair, a row of pots behind me, shining,
some gold leaking out from the kitchen.

HAIL MARY

Oh Immaculate Heart of Mary, Heart
of the Woods, the Invisible Deer, the Woodsman,
his Axe, his Leaf Blower. Oh Flawless Heart
of the North Wind, the Frosted grass, the Tattered
Curtains. Oh Tidy Heart of Kate and Grace
        Light our way Home!

There are layers of dirt under petticoats
between the wood and city, cobwebs and curtains.
They have hunted, gathered, chopped wood, scrubbed
floors, black leaded stoves, whitened hearths,
slaked dust and swept and wept. They are no angels
and know the woodsmen and plasterers' low slung ways.

Oh Tidy Heart of Kate and Grace, Heart
of our Mother, of all our Dead, and Us
sliding down the wooded slope, England's Glory
        Light our way Home!

XII

Return With Elixir

IN THEIR LITTLE LOST ROAD

In the road by the park, the trees all in bud
the air clean with renewal – the first time.
The second time, clambering lamblike up
the steep path to mistress the trees
the box so juicy, the birds so noisy.
I am never in a wood again without the child.

BACK ON THE MARSH (AGAIN)

Songs drift out along with the smell of bluebells
and woodbine. They drift along the alleyway
where once sheep grazed. They come out and knock
on the door saying 'is so and so there?'

another voice says *I don't know love,*
but come in anyway! They are forever
rolling out their barrel. The piano in the corner
the flowers in a milk bottle hover happy
as marsh ghosts on a Saturday night.

RESURRECTING THE CHAIR

We are holding the webbing taut, as taut
as we can, while Uncle Vic hammers five
tacks to each end of the web. We've stripped
the chair, ripped it back to the wood. Placed
new springs. The new brown velvet waits its turn.
There's a smell in the air of a workshop,
sawdust and tea; although really no sawdust.

We're in the living room, on the Marsh.
This chair needs a sacrifice, something
to keep it sure in its purpose. I wrap,
in a linen cloth, a small book of stories.
On the cover is a wood, a woodsman,
in between the trees, a small dirty girl;
we place it in the seat and web it in.

MAGIC FOLLOWS ONLY THE FEW.

There's a red admiral. How it appeared
in this room, I don't know.
Windows locked, door closed
against the cold of autumn.
Maybe it came down the chimney,
or maybe from you, that sign of her –
your familiar and daemon, as she
breathed her last, a bit before
you breathed yours. At first when
I open the window, it seems reluctant
to fly, but then catching the breeze,
is off, into the yard, faster
than you could whisper *Into the Forest*.